OTHER BOOKS IN THIS SERIES

8 PEOPLE MEET JESUS

8 SURPRISES AND STORIES BY JESUS

amazon

8
QUESTIONS AND ANSWERS BY JESUS

BEVERLEY BOISSERY

PACKER PUBLICATIONS

CONTENTS

This book in the LEARN ABOUT JESUS series is inspired by Sandy Harmel and her ESL Bible Study group at St. John's Vancouver church. We are very grateful for their encouragement, comments and suggestions.

STUDY TIPS

How to get the most out of these studies:

1. Do each study before you meet as a group.

2. Ask God to help you understand what you read. If you are new to prayer, you might like the say the following:

God, help me understand what I read. Help me understand what it tells about you and your son, Jesus. Help me to take the message in these words into my heart. Amen

3. Use a modern translation of the Bible. We usually quote from the New International Version, so that might be a good translation to use.

4. Find a quiet spot with as few distractions as possible.

5. Turn off your cell phone.

6. Don't worry if you can't find an answer to a question — mark it and go on to the next one. Remember to ask about it in your group session.

7. NEVER be afraid to ask questions. Jesus was very willing to answer them. If you don't understand, always ask for help.

SESSION 1

JESUS TALKS ABOUT NOW AND THEN – LUKE 12: 13-21

[13] Someone in the crowd said to him, "Teacher, tell my brother to divide the inheritance with me."

[14] Jesus replied, "Man, who appointed me a judge or an arbiter between you?" [15] Then he said to them, "Watch out! Be on your guard against all kinds of greed; life does not consist in an abundance of possessions."

[16] And he told them this parable: "The ground of a certain rich man yielded an abundant harvest. [17] He thought to himself, 'What shall I do? I have no place to store my crops.'

[18] "Then he said, 'This is what I'll do. I will tear down my barns and build bigger ones, and there I will store my surplus grain. [19] And I'll say to myself, "You have plenty of grain laid up for many years. Take life easy; eat, drink and be merry."'

[20] "But God said to him, 'You fool! This very night your life will be demanded from you. Then who will get what you have prepared for yourself?'

[21] "This is how it will be with whoever stores up things for themselves but is not rich toward God."

Once Jesus became famous, crowds came to hear him speak. On one such occasion he spoke from a ledge on a hill. This talk later became known as "The Sermon from the Mount."

People had all kinds of questions for Jesus. About life and its meaning, and sometimes they asked, as we'll see, about the much more ordinary.

1. What is the demand made in verse 13? What does the person ask Jesus to do?

2. Why do you think the questioner asked Jesus to do this?

3. What can you guess about the person's values?

4. Instead of saying yes or no, what does Jesus warn his questioner about?

As we will see in this and the next study, Jesus is more concerned about the future than the present. A poor analogy would be him talking to people at an airport. He'd be asking questions about WHERE they're going and about HOW they're preparing themselves for when they get there rather than ordinary questions like where he could get coffee.

5. Jesus tells a story in verses 16-18. Summarize it in your own words.

6. Think about how Jesus might change the barn image to make it work if he were talking to us. How might he tell the same story, but with the different images, today?

7. How does God react in verse 20? Why do you think he reacts that way?

8. Look at the last three words of the passage – "rich towards God." What do you suppose Jesus means when he says them?

9. What does "rich towards God" mean in your life?

10. What do you think the person who asked the question in verse 13 thought about the answer Jesus gave?

God isn't against saving for the future or having a wonderful old age. That isn't the purpose of the man with a barn story. God is concerned about us and our values as we work and save towards the future though. The following quotation is from Emily Carr is Canada's most famous female artist. When she began getting old, she wrote that she said to herself:

> *"I must hurry because the years crowd by so quickly I have little working time left. Fool. Time is God's. You will have just as long as He intends you to have, all the time and all the opportunity He wills. You and your work are not so important as you think.*
>
> *The only thing that is important is God."*

Although she was a theist, Emily Carr understood the lesson Jesus taught that long ago day in his Sermon from the Mount. Instead of fretting about the masterpieces she might or might not have time to paint, she looked forward to the time she would see God in heaven.

She sought the kingdom of God. He was the only important thing in her life. Do you think the same way?

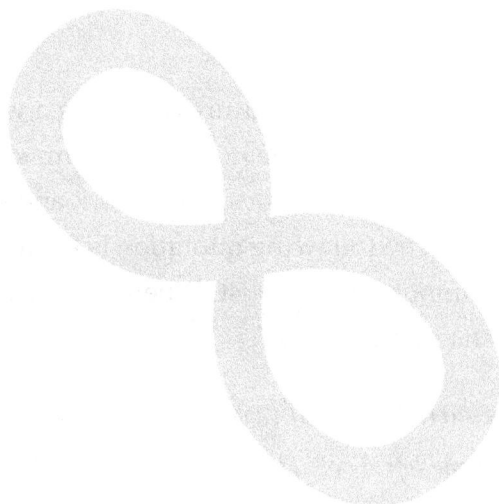

SESSION 2

JESUS TALKS ABOUT WORRY – LUKE 12: 22-34

[22] Then Jesus said to his disciples: "Therefore I tell you, do not worry about your life, what you will eat; or about your body, what you will wear. [23] For life is more than food, and the body more than clothes. [24] Consider the ravens: They do not sow or reap, they have no storeroom or barn; yet God feeds them. And how much more valuable you are than birds! [25] Who of you by worrying can add a single hour to your life[a]? [26] Since you cannot do this very little thing, why do you worry about the rest?

[27] "Consider how the wild flowers grow. They do not labor or spin. Yet I tell you, not even Solomon in all his splendor was dressed like one of these. [28] If that is how God clothes the grass of the field, which is here today, and tomorrow is thrown into the fire, how much more will he clothe you—you of little faith! [29] And do not set your heart on what you will eat or drink; do not worry about it. [30] For the pagan world runs after all such things, and your Father knows that you need them. [31] But seek his kingdom, and these things will be given to you as well.

[32] "Do not be afraid, little flock, for your Father has been pleased to give you the kingdom. [33] Sell your possessions and give to the poor. Provide purses for yourselves that will not wear out, a treasure in heaven that will never fail, where no thief comes near

7

and no moth destroys. ^{34} For where your treasure is, there your heart will be also.

Life is full of worry, stress and anxiety. In many parts of the world, people worry about having enough food to feed their families and how to get safe housing. Many of us take life's basics for granted. It's one of life's ironies though, that it seems that the more we have, the more we want, and the more we worry.

Jesus knew people like us. He saw them worrying and stressing and after the previous story, he talked about it. He is concerned about our destination. He talks about the now and then, about life and life after death, and, about preparing for our eventual destination.

1. What do you worry about most in life? Think about it and write down three of your main worries.

2. What does Jesus ask in verse 25?

3. What's his follow-up question in verse 26?

4. If you could talk to Jesus face to face, if you were part of that group he was talking to, what would you say to him?

5. Now go back to verse 24, the place where Jesus sets up his questions. He says the ravens don't seem to work, but God feeds them anyway. But what's the real point he's making here?

6. In verse 28, Jesus uses another seemingly valueless thing from nature next—wild flowers. He compares them and their glorious flowers to Solomon, the richest king in Jewish history, and who was known for his conspicuous consumption. Read through to verse 31 and, again, work out the real thing Jesus is saying.

7. Do you feel loved by God? How has God blessed you? What gifts in your life would you say came from God?

8. What does seeking the kingdom of God mean? How do people go about that?

9. When you think about God, do you think about him as your Father? What does that look like in real life? What does it look life in your life?

10. What does Jesus say is the real difference between our treasures here on earth and treasure in heaven?

11. Verse 34 says that our hearts are where are treasure is. Think deeply and honestly. If Jesus asked what were your goals and priorities, what would you tell him?

Sometimes the things Jesus says seem impossible. But he knew that people are burdened by worry. We fret, we stress about money, global warming, staying healthy, getting our kids into the right schools. The list is endless.

Jesus saw people around him just like us. Worry and anxiety made life something to endure, because they certainly weren't enjoying it. As always, he told them to look to God, his Father and our Father.

And that's what makes this passage from the famous Sermon on the Mount so tricky. At first glance, Jesus seems to be telling us not to worry about feeding or clothing ourselves. But we know from other parts of the Bible, that we are expected to feed and clothe ourselves. So what is he really saying?

Imagine yourself going to a great party. You think out what you're going to wear and how you're going to get there. You stress about having the right clothes or the right transportation and you forget all about the purpose of what you're doing. To a little extent, this is what is saying. We're so obsessed with what we're doing that we forget about heaven and our heavenly Father. We're so busy acquiring stuff that we sometimes don't leave room to see God's blessings. Even worse, we put our faith in the treasures we can get for ourselves and not the ones that will be eternal.

In another words, we're trusting ourselves and not God. No wonder life seems nothing but toil and trouble, worry and anxiety. The good news that Jesus told that long ago day was that, if we order our priorities so that God and his kingdom are number one, God will give us all we need. Not all that we want. But, definitely, all that we need.

SESSION 3

JESUS TALKS ABOUT HEAVEN & HAPPINESS – LUKE 15: 1-10

1 Now the tax collectors and sinners were all gathering around to hear Jesus. [2] But the Pharisees and the teachers of the law muttered, "This man welcomes sinners and eats with them."

[3] Then Jesus told them this parable: [4] "Suppose one of you has a hundred sheep and loses one of them. Doesn't he leave the ninety-nine in the open country and go after the lost sheep until he finds it? [5] And when he finds it, he joyfully puts it on his shoulders [6] and goes home. Then he calls his friends and neighbors together and says, 'Rejoice with me; I have found my lost sheep.' [7] I tell you that in the same way there will be more rejoicing in heaven over one sinner who repents than over ninety-nine righteous persons who do not need to repent.

[8] "Or suppose a woman has ten silver coins[a] and loses one. Doesn't she light a lamp, sweep the house and search carefully until she finds it? [9] And when she finds it, she calls her friends and neighbors together and says, 'Rejoice with me; I have found my lost coin.' [10] In the same way, I tell you, there is rejoicing in the presence of the angels of God over one sinner who repents."

Jesus lived in a land controlled by the Romans. Roman soldiers patrolled the roads, taxes were paid to Rome, and a Roman governor lived in a palace in Jerusalem. The real leaders of his society, though, were an elite made up of religious leaders called the Pharisees, the chief priests, and lawyers who interpreted the

Jewish law. As their power centered on them being the ones who controlled access to God, they took an increasingly intense and hostile interest in Jesus. He spoke about the Kingdom of God to everyone—even those the elite despised and called sinners.

Jesus, of course, knew that everyone sins. In the last couple of studies he's told us to look heavenwards and to God. In these two stories, he gives us, and those who called everyone else sinners, a glimpse of heaven and what makes it happy.

1. Jesus tells these stories to ordinary people. If he were telling the story in verses 3-6 nowadays, what changes might he make?

2. Who did Jesus tell this story to? What is his point?

3. We call people like the religious elite "hypocritical." In another confrontation, Jesus tells them to see their own mistakes before they criticize others. Think about this story and then, of course, put it into our own world. In your opinion, who are today's equivalent of the religious elite of Jesus' time?

4. The next story is about a woman who is relatively poor. The silver coins Jesus speaks about represented about two weeks' salary. So when she lost that one silver coin, it meant losing what she had earned doing a day's work. Again, try to put the story into today's context. What would make you search high and low when you lost it?

5. Now, think about God. What has he lost?

6. What must happen for the "lost" to be found, according to Jesus?

7. Are you one of the lost, or have you been found? If you're still lost, what do you have to do to be found? What, if anything is stopping you from telling God you've been wrong (in Biblical language, you have sinned) and that you want to come home?

8. What happens when God finds what He's lost?

9. Have you ever thought of yourself as being that valuable? Does it help you understand why Jesus had to die on the cross for us?

10. In Sessions 1 and 2, Jesus directed our thoughts heavenwards. He told us not to put all our emphases on this life, because it wouldn't last. The mighty Roman empire of the time of Jesus didn't last, and few people know or care about the religious elite of verse 2. So that's why Jesus told us to think about heaven and about things that are forever.

This Session takes us a step further. If we repent, we will be one of those people who live forever with God who looks for us when we are lost and rejoices when He finds us. How have these sessions changed, if at all, your thinking about God and things that won't change, the eternal things?

SESSION 4

JESUS TALKS ABOUT SIN – LUKE 7: 36-48

---

[36] When one of the Pharisees invited Jesus to have dinner with him, he went to the Pharisee's house and reclined at the table. [37] A woman in that town who lived a sinful life learned that Jesus was eating at the Pharisee's house, so she came there with an alabaster jar of perfume. [38] As she stood behind him at his feet weeping, she began to wet his feet with her tears. Then she wiped them with her hair, kissed them and poured perfume on them.

[39] When the Pharisee who had invited him saw this, he said to himself, "If this man were a prophet, he would know who is touching him and what kind of woman she is—that she is a sinner."

[40] Jesus answered him, "Simon, I have something to tell you."

"Tell me, teacher," he said.

[41] "Two people owed money to a certain moneylender. One owed him five hundred denarii,[a] and the other fifty. [42] Neither of them had the money to pay him back, so he forgave the debts of both. Now which of them will love him more?"

[43] Simon replied, "I suppose the one who had the bigger debt forgiven."

"You have judged correctly," Jesus said.

[44] Then he turned toward the woman and said to Simon, "Do you see this woman? I came into your house. You did not give me any water for my feet, but she wet my feet with her tears and wiped them with her hair. [45] You did not give me a kiss, but this woman, from the time I entered,

has not stopped kissing my feet. [46] You did not put oil on my head, but she has poured perfume on my feet. [47] Therefore, I tell you, her many sins have been forgiven—as her great love has shown. But whoever has been forgiven little loves little."

[48] Then Jesus said to her, "Your sins are forgiven."

This is a story about great love and one of the problems with sin. One problem when we think about sin is that we think about it the same way we think about crime. If we break traffic laws, we are usually fined. If we commit a major crime, we are sent to jail for many years. God, however, doesn't have degrees of sin. He is holy and sin, no matter how small, is abhorrent to him. This is one of the lessons from this story. Sin is sin.

1. Think about what you learned about the Pharisees in lesson 3. Who was Simon? Why might he have asked Jesus for dinner?

2. The dinner was gate-crashed by a woman Simon calls a "sinner." She probably worked in the sex trade. List what did she does when she meets Jesus at the dinner.

3. In Simon's time, the word "prophet" usually meant someone who received his information from God. Given this definition, what is Simon really thinking in verse 39?

4. Read verses 41 and 42 carefully. If Jesus had asked you the question in verse 42, how would you have answered it?

A denarius was roughly a day's salary. Today, we are used to the concept of relativism. We think about the man who owed the five hundred denarii. He must have been rich to have been lent that much—a year and a half's salary. We think about the other man who'd been lent only fifty denarii. Obviously, he was much poorer. And so, we sometimes get confused by this question. But now, let's leave it with the way Simon answered the question.

5. Jesus uses the question to begin to teach Simon about sin. Simon, after all, had asked Jesus for dinner, but what had he failed to do?

6. When Jesus lived most people wore sandals and walked with household and animal waste in the streets. Once they went inside a house, their feet were usually washed by a slave. Simon neglected to have this done for Jesus. How do you interpret this and the other signs of neglect?

7. Why is the woman's behavior such a contrast to Simon's?

8. By her behavior, the woman showed her complete love for Jesus. Alabaster was a precious stone. Flasks or jars carved from it would stop perfume or oils from evaporating until they were used. Estimates for the "ointment" (probably anointing oil or perfume) range from a half year to a full year's salary. It was indeed a very costly gift for a woman who earned her way in life in the sex trade. What do you sacrifice to show your love for Jesus? If you don't, what might make you do so?

God, of course, is our model here. In Session 3, you learned that he values each of us so much that heaven rejoices when we repent of our sin. But we have an even bigger example of God's love. Like the woman in this story, his love is sacrificial. He sent Jesus to live among us, to have his feet stained with garbage and excrement, and then to die a horrible death on the cross.

9. Why did Jesus have to be crucified?

10. Do you truly understand how much God loves you? Do you really know now how valuable you are to him?

SESSION 5

JESUS ASKS ABOUT HIS IDENTITY
– MARK 8: 22-30

[22] They came to Bethsaida, and some people brought a blind man and begged Jesus to touch him. [23] He took the blind man by the hand and led him outside the village. When he had spit on the man's eyes and put his hands on him, Jesus asked, "Do you see anything?"

[24] He looked up and said, "I see people; they look like trees walking around."

[25] Once more Jesus put his hands on the man's eyes. Then his eyes were opened, his sight was restored, and he saw everything clearly. [26] Jesus sent him home, saying, "Don't even go into[a] the village."

[27] Jesus and his disciples went on to the villages around Caesarea Philippi. On the way he asked them, "Who do people say I am?"

[28] They replied, "Some say John the Baptist; others say Elijah; and still others, one of the prophets."

[29] "But what about you?" he asked. "Who do you say I am?"

Peter answered, "You are the Messiah."

[30] Jesus warned them not to tell anyone about him.

1. Concentrate on verses 22-25 in which Jesus heals a blind man. What is the differences between the sight the man gets in verse 24 and that in verse 25?

2. What is he told not to do?

3. Why do you think Jesus said this?

4. Now read verses 27-30. What is Jesus curious about?

BACKGROUND INFORMATION: John the Baptist was born a few months before Jesus. He was a respected prophet who told people to look for Jesus. Elijah was also a prophet, but he lived more than 800 years before Jesus. He did miraculous things and defended God.

5. What, then, are the crowds saying about Jesus?

6. Why do you think people answered the way they did in verse 28?

7. How does Peter answer the question about the identity of Jesus?

The word "Messiah" that Peter uses in verse 29 is very important. It comes from the Old Testament and could also be translated as "Christ." Peter, therefore, answers that he believes that Jesus is special, that he's the son of God and God's choice for our eternal king.

God's special, chosen, eternal king and son

8. Think back to the story about the blind man. One thing you should know is that the Bible is a carefully crafted work, and that Mark would have thought long and hard about placing the story of the blind man right before the story centering on the identity of Jesus. What connections do you see between verses 22-26 and verses 27-30?

9. Imagine that Jesus is in your group and he asked, "Who do your friends and the people you know think I am?" What would you tell him?

10. Now, go to the next step. Imagine Jesus then turns to you and asks, "Who do you think I am?" How would you answer?

SESSION 6

JESUS TALKS ABOUT DEATH AND THE FUTURE – MARK 8: 31-38

[31] He then began to teach them that the Son of Man must suffer many things and be rejected by the elders, the chief priests and the teachers of the law, and that he must be killed and after three days rise again. [32] He spoke plainly about this, and Peter took him aside and began to rebuke him.

[33] But when Jesus turned and looked at his disciples, he rebuked Peter. "Get behind me, Satan!" he said. "You do not have in mind the concerns of God, but merely human concerns."

[34] Then he called the crowd to him along with his disciples and said: "Whoever wants to be my disciple must deny themselves and take up their cross and follow me. [35] For whoever wants to save their life[a] will lose it, but whoever loses their life for me and for the gospel will save it. [36] What good is it for someone to gain the whole world, yet forfeit their soul? [37] Or what can anyone give in exchange for their soul? [38] If anyone is ashamed of me and my words in this adulterous and sinful generation, the Son of Man will

be ashamed of them when he comes in his Father's glory with the holy angels."

It seems so sad and ironic that Mark follows the previous story with this one. Once again, remember that he would have done this only after much thought and prayer. In a short period of time, the disciples have witnessed the blind man made able to see and Peter declare that Jesus was the Messiah.

God had promised to send a Messiah for hundreds of years. This messiah would restore purity to a decaying world. People looked for the messiah everywhere and many fake ones had crowds follow them. By the time Jesus lived, many people expected that the messiah would free them from Rome and, as we shall see in this session, Jesus did not fit into their expectations.

1. What does Jesus predict about his death?

2. Why do you think Peter reacted so strongly to what Jesus said?

3. Jesus is harsh when he responds to Peter. Why do you think that is?

4. Read verses 34-38 carefully and think about them. What, exactly, does Jesus challenge people to do if they want to follow him?

When Jesus lived, the worst way to die was by being nailed to a cross. It was extraordinarily painful, it took a long time to die. To make it worse, people threw anything they could find at those sentenced dying in this horrible way.

5. Now think about our world. Are there fake messiahs in it? If so, why do we follow them?

6. What would it mean to take our "our cross" today? Jesus still tells us to do it. How many "likes" do you think he gets with this strategy?

7. Have you noticed that Jesus is going back to the themes we studied in Sessions 1 and 2? Again he challenges people to look further than this world's problems personal goals. What are the two questions he asks the crowd?

8. The theme of people losing their souls or mortgaging them is a popular one in literature, music and the movies. Can you think of one or two?

9. What do people "sell" their souls for? Is there anything that might make you think of doing so?

10. According to Jesus, what must you do to get eternal life in heaven?

Are you willing to do this?

SESSION 7

JESUS CONSENTS TO DIE – JOHN 18:28-40; 19: 1-16

[28] Then the Jewish leaders took Jesus from Caiaphas to the palace of the Roman governor. By now it was early morning, and to avoid ceremonial uncleanness they did not enter the palace, because they wanted to be able to eat the Passover. [29] So Pilate came out to them and asked, "What charges are you bringing against this man?"

[30] "If he were not a criminal," they replied, "we would not have handed him over to you."

[31] Pilate said, "Take him yourselves and judge him by your own law."

"But we have no right to execute anyone," they objected. [32] This took place to fulfill what Jesus had said about the kind of death he was going to die.

[33] Pilate then went back inside the palace, summoned Jesus and asked him, "Are you the king of the Jews?"

[34] "Is that your own idea," Jesus asked, "or did others talk to you about me?"

[35] "Am I a Jew?" Pilate replied. "Your own people and chief priests handed you over to me. What is it you have done?"

[36] Jesus said, "My kingdom is not of this world. If it were, my servants would fight to prevent my arrest by the Jewish leaders. But now my kingdom is from another place."

[37] "You are a king, then!" said Pilate.

Jesus answered, "You say that I am a king. In fact, the reason I was born and came into the world is to testify to the truth. Everyone on the side of truth listens to me."

[38] "What is truth?" retorted Pilate. With this he went out again to the Jews gathered there and said, "I find no basis for a charge against him. [39] But it is your custom for me to release to you one prisoner at the time of the Passover. Do you want me to release 'the king of the Jews'?"

[40] They shouted back, "No, not him! Give us Barabbas!" Now Barabbas had taken part in an uprising.

19 Then Pilate took Jesus and had him flogged. [2] The soldiers twisted together a crown of thorns and put it on his head. They clothed him in a purple robe [3] and went up to him again and again, saying, "Hail, king of the Jews!" And they slapped him in the face.

[4] Once more Pilate came out and said to the Jews gathered there, "Look, I am bringing him out to you to let you know that I find no basis for a charge against him." [5] When Jesus came out wearing the crown of thorns and the purple robe, Pilate said to them, "Here is the man!"

[6] As soon as the chief priests and their officials saw him, they shouted, "Crucify! Crucify!" But Pilate answered, "You take him

and crucify him. As for me, I find no basis for a charge against him."

[7] The Jewish leaders insisted, "We have a law, and according to that law he must die, because he claimed to be the Son of God."

[8] When Pilate heard this, he was even more afraid, [9] and he went back inside the palace. "Where do you come from?" he asked Jesus, but Jesus gave him no answer. [10] "Do you refuse to speak to me?" Pilate said. "Don't you realize I have power either to free you or to crucify you?"

[11] Jesus answered, "You would have no power over me if it were not given to you from above. Therefore the one who handed me over to you is guilty of a greater sin."

[12] From then on, Pilate tried to set Jesus free, but the Jewish leaders kept shouting, "If you let this man go, you are no friend of Caesar. Anyone who claims to be a king opposes Caesar."

[13] When Pilate heard this, he brought Jesus out and sat down on the judge's seat at a place known as the Stone Pavement (which in Aramaic is Gabbatha). [14] It was the day of Preparation of the Passover; it was about noon.

"Here is your king," Pilate said to the Jews.

[15] But they shouted, "Take him away! Take him away! Crucify him!"

"Shall I crucify your king?" Pilate asked.

"We have no king but Caesar," the chief priests answered.

[16] Finally Pilate handed him over to them to be crucified.

So the soldiers took charge of Jesus.

Earlier we saw how suspicious the Pharisees were. Now we see that they were determined that Jesus had to die. The chief priest, Caiaphas, arranged for Jesus to be arrested. But, the only way they could have him executed would need a trial by the Roman governor, Pilate. In this tragic scene Jesus is dragged to Pilate's palace.

Caiaphas put Pilate in an impossible position. Jesus is a religious problem, not a military or political one. Yet Caiaphas demands that Pilate find Jesus guilty of something and execute him immediately.

1. From this passage, what kind of person do you think Pilate is?

2. In verse 36, what does Jesus say is the difference between a kingdom on earth and the Kingdom of God?

3. We see Pilate trying to understand the crime Jesus is accused of in verse 37 to the first sentence in verse 38. He must have found it difficult because Jesus shifts from explaining kingdoms to asking about the essence of truth. If Pilate asked you the question in verse 38, "What is truth?" what would you answer?

4. In the rest of verse 38 to verse 40, we see Pilate's first desperate attempt to save Jesus. By tradition, the Jews had a right to play a "Get out of jail free" card. Once a year they could choose to save someone sentenced to death. What does Pilate tell them?

5. Why do you think they chose Barabbas, a rebel against Rome, to be freed instead of Jesus? What more does this tell us about the religious elite of Pharisees and priests?

6. Why do you think Pilate orders that Jesus be flogged and allows him to be humiliated (chapter 19, verses 1-6)?

7. After all this, though, Pilate tries again to save Jesus from death on the cross. What do the people reveal as the real reason they want Jesus dead in verse 7?

8. Centuries earlier, the prophet Isaiah wrote about the death of the promised Messiah. Find Isaiah 53, verses 1-7, in the Old Testament part of the Bible. Maybe someone in your group can read it aloud. Using this background, why do you think Jesus doesn't answer Pilate anymore?

9. Read Pilate's last attempt to save Jesus in verse 15 and think hard about the last answer the chief priests give him. It's one of the Bible's biggest ironies that the priests and Pharisees, the self-appointed guardians to the kingdom of God, would choose the Roman emperor as their king. What does this show about their values?

10. Although this is such a difficult story, the theme is the same as it's been in the previous studies. It's about what we value and work for in this life. The religious elite's interest in their wealth and power in this life prevented them from seeing God's son and their real king. They chose life now rather than heaven.

The thing is that God loves us so much that he allowed these horrible things to happen to his son so that we might have that life in heaven. We've seen how valuable we are to him. Now we know how much we cost—the death of Jesus. Has Jesus convinced you yet to think about heaven and follow him?

SESSION 8

JESUS DIES TO GIVE US LIFE –
LUKE 23: 32-49

[32] Two other men, both criminals, were also led out with him to be executed. [33] When they came to the place called the Skull, they crucified him there, along with the criminals — one on his right, the other on his left. [34] Jesus said, "Father, forgive them, for they do not know what they are doing." And they divided up his clothes by casting lots.

[35] The people stood watching, and the rulers even **sneered** at him. They said, "He saved others; let him save himself if he is God's Messiah, the Chosen One." [36] The soldiers also came up and **mocked** him. They offered him wine vinegar [37] and said, "If you are the king of the Jews, save yourself." [38] There was a written notice above him, which read: THIS IS THE KING OF THE JEWS.

[39] One of the criminals who hung there **hurled** insults at him: "Aren't you the Messiah? Save yourself and us!" [40] But the other criminal rebuked him. "Don't you fear God," he said, "since you are under the same sentence? [41] We are punished justly, for we are getting what our deeds deserve. But this man has done nothing wrong." [42] Then he said, "Jesus, remember me when you come into your kingdom." [43] Jesus answered him, "Truly I tell you, today you will be with me in paradise."

[44] It was now about noon, and darkness came over the whole land until three in the afternoon, [45] for the sun stopped shining. And the curtain of the temple was torn in two. [46] Jesus called out with a loud voice, "Father, into your hands I commit my spirit."[c] When he had said this, he breathed his last.

[47] The centurion, seeing what had happened, praised God and said, "Surely this was a righteous man." [48] When all the people who had gathered to witness this sight saw what took place, they beat their breasts and went away. [49] But all those who knew him, including the women who had followed him from Galilee, stood at a distance, watching these things.

1. Look at the three bolded verbs in verses 35-39. What sense do you get of the atmosphere of the crucifixion from these words?

2. What are people taunting Jesus to do in these verses?

3. Read verse 40. What insight does the second criminal have that the first doesn't?

BACKGROUND:

The curtain, referred to in verse 45, was about sixty feet (18m) high and thirty feet (9.1m) wide. It was made of 72 braids, with 24 threads in each braid. It would have been impossible for anybody to have torn it into two from top to bottom.

4. Remember the stories about heaven rejoicing when people repent of their sins and accept this terrible sacrifice Jesus made? Remember being asked about God seeing you as valuable?

Using your own knowledge about how you would feel if Jesus was your son and the evidence in this passage, what can you tell about God's emotions as He watched his only and very well-loved son die in this way?

5. To the best of your knowledge, how is the death of Jesus different from that of other great religious leaders?

6. The centurion was a Roman officer in charge of 100 men. He had probably seen everything that had happened to Jesus at Pilate's palace and certainly seen everything that happened at the place called the Skull. What do you think factored into what he said in verse 47?

7. Mark wrote in his Gospel (chapter 10, verse 45: "For even the Son of Man did not come to be served, but to serve, and to give his life as a ransom for many." Why do you think Jesus had to die?

8. Why couldn't Jesus save both himself and us?

9. Remember learning about Kingdom of God? The whole trial and execution of Jesus was about him being the "King of the Jews." Read verse 48. In the time of Jesus, beating (or thumping) breasts was a sign of grief and repentance. Do you think these people finally understood that Jesus was indeed their king? Why or why not?

10. This entire series of studies has been about looking towards your future. It's been about building real treasure by seeking the Kingdom of God. You've seen that heaven becomes extremely happy when a single person repents of their sin and accepts that Jesus has made things right for them with God. That's what ransom means in question 7.

You've learned that you have great value. Now you've read about the high ransom price Jesus paid so that you can enjoy a forever life with him and his father in Heaven. God and Jesus have done their part to bring this about. The only thing that can stop you having eternal life in the Kingdom of God is you, and all you have to do is ask God to forgive your sins.

In the end, it all comes down to what you think about Jesus. There's only three possible ways to make sense of him. Either he was **mad** (delusional) with his talk of being the messiah and the son of God, or he was **bad** and a fraud, or he was really who he said – the Son of God who died to ransom us.

The great 20ᵗʰ century writer C.S. Lewis (of *The Lion, The Witch and The Wardrobe* fame) put it far more cleverly. He said we choose to look at Jesus as either a lunatic, a liar, or our Lord.

So, that's it. There are three choices. Which do you choose?

ABOUT THE AUTHOR

BEV BOISSERY was born in Sydney, Australia and earned her doctorate at the Australian National University. She now lives in Vancouver and attends the same church as her friend, Bron. Bev has written twenty books, ranging from academic history to Bible Studies. She is mainly known for her award-winning Young Adult fiction.